TOUGH
QUESTIONS...
REAL ANSWERS
ABOUT
GRIEF

SMITH FREEMAN
Publishing

Tough Questions...Real Answers About Homosexuality

Bible verses were taken from the following translations:

KJV: The Holy Bible, King James Version

HCSB: Scripture quotations marked HCSB® are taken from the Holman Christian Standard Bible®, Copyright © 1999, 2000, 2002, 2003, 2009 by Holman Bible Publishers. Used by permission. HCSB® is a federally registered trademark of Holman Bible Publishers.

ICB: The Holy Bible, International Children's Bible® Copyright © 1986, 1988, 1999, 2015 by Tommy Nelson™, a division of Thomas Nelson. Thomas Nelson is a registered trademark of Harper Collins Christian Publishing, Inc.

NASB: Scripture quotations taken from the New American Standard Bible®, Copyright © 1960, 1962, 1963, 1968, 1971, 1972, 1973, 1975, 1977, 1995 by The Lockman Foundation. Used by permission.

NCV: Scripture taken from the New Century Version. Copyright © 1987, 1988, 1991 by Thomas Nelson, Inc. Used by permission. All rights reserved.

NIV: THE HOLY BIBLE, NEW INTERNATIONAL VERSION® NIV® Copyright © 1973, 1978, 1984 by International Bible Society® Used by permission. All rights reserved worldwide.

NKJV: Scripture taken from the New King James Version. Copyright © 1982 by Thomas Nelson, Inc. Used by permission. All rights reserved.

NLT: Holy Bible, New Living Translation, copyright © 1996, 2004, 2007 by Tyndale House Foundation. Used by permission of Tyndale House Publishers, Inc. All rights reserved.

ISBN 978-0-9986529-1-7

Contents

A Message to Readers

God's Word promises that all things work together for the good of those who love Him. Yet sometimes we encounter circumstances that seem so troubling—or so tragic—that we simply cannot understand how these events might be a part of God's plan for our lives. We experience a deeply significant loss: perhaps the death of a loved one; perhaps the loss of health; perhaps divorce, job loss, or a broken personal relationship. Whatever the nature of the loss, its pain is so profound that we honestly wonder if recovery is possible. But with God, all things are possible.

The Christian faith, as communicated through the words of the Holy Bible, is a healing faith. It offers comfort in times of trouble, courage to allay our fears, hope instead of hopelessness. For Christians, the grave is not a final destination; it is a place of transition. Through the healing words of God's promises, Christians understand that the Lord continues to manifest His plan in good times and in hard times.

If you are experiencing the intense pain of a recent loss, or if you are still mourning a loss from long ago, this book is intended to help. The ideas contained on these pages are intended to remind you that your suffering is temporary but God's love is eternal. When you weave His promises into the fabric of your day, you'll quickly discover that His Word has the power to change everything, including you.

Grief is not meant to be avoided or feared; it is meant to be worked through. If this text assists you even in a small way, as you move through and beyond your pain, it will have served its purpose. May God bless you and keep you, now and forever. And may He place His healing hand upon your heart today.

Seven Things to Remember
as You Walk through—
and Work through—Your Grief

God Is Always with You. He never leaves your side for an instant, not even for a moment. You can take comfort in that fact.

Recovery Is Possible. If you think you'll never recover, you're wrong. With God, all things are possible. Ask and you will receive.

Recovery Takes Time. Don't expect healing to take place overnight. Do expect healing to take place over time.

It Helps to Express Your Pain. Don't keep your feelings bottled up inside. By honestly expressing your grief, you will take an active role in God's plan for your recovery.

It Helps to Make Peace with Your Past. Focus on the future; accept the things you cannot change; forgive everybody; and move on.

God's Word Provides Comfort and Assurance. If you're grieving, you need a daily appointment with God. When you give Him your undivided attention, everything changes, including you.

Your Pain Is Temporary; God's Love Is Eternal. Your heavenly Father has the power to make all things new, including you.

1

The Question

My feelings of sadness are so intense.
How can I deal with them?

The Answer

When your pain is intense, you should
remember that with time—and with God—
your heart will heal. It's helpful to remember
that grief is a process, a process that
you will eventually work through.

Grief is the aftermath of any deeply significant loss.
WAYNE OATES

Understanding Grief

Blessed are the poor in spirit:
for theirs is the kingdom of heaven.
Blessed are they that mourn:
for they shall be comforted.

MATTHEW 5:3–4 KJV

Grief is a profoundly personal experience. But grief is also a universal experience, a journey that has been mapped time and again by those who have documented the common elements of human suffering.

Grief often begins with shock and then gives way to intense pain. Over time, as the mourner slowly begins to regain his or her emotional balance, the pain begins to fade. Gradually—sometimes almost imperceptibly—a new life is raised from the ashes of the old. And even though the mourner may never "get over" his losses, he can eventually move beyond the intensity of the initial pain. Some losses are, of course, so profound and so painful that a mourner is forever changed, but for followers of Christ, the experience of grief is different in one very important respect: Christians face grief armed with God's promises.

Through the Bible, God promises to comfort and heal those who call upon Him. And He promises that the grave need not be a final resting place; it is, instead, merely a place of transition—a way station on the path to eternal life for those who give their hearts to God's Son.

As you consider the ideas in this book, think carefully about your own situation: your thoughts, your emotions, your experiences, and your pain. And think carefully about the ways that you're responding to your own particular loses. The more you understand about the grieving process—and the more you understand about your own particular grieving process—the better you can cope with its many twists and turns. But whatever the nature of your loss, always remember this overriding truth: God is with you, God is good, and you are protected.

More from God's Word

He heals the brokenhearted
and binds up their wounds.
PSALM 147:3 HCSB

Weeping may endure for a night,
but joy cometh in the morning.
PSALM 30:5 KJV

The LORD shall give thee rest from thy sorrow,
and from thy fear.
ISAIAH 14:3 KJV

The LORD is near to those who have a broken heart.
PSALM 34:18 NKJV

Ye shall be sorrowful,
but your sorrow shall be turned into joy.
JOHN 16:20 KJV

More Thoughts About Grief

God is sufficient for all our needs,
for every problem, for every difficulty, for every
broken heart, for every human sorrow.
PETER MARSHALL

Your greatest ministry will most likely
come out of your greatest hurt.
RICK WARREN

If there is something we need more than anything
else during grief, it is a friend who stands with us,
who doesn't leave us. Jesus is that friend.
BILLY GRAHAM

God has enough grace to solve every dilemma
you face, wipe every tear you cry,
and answer every question you ask.
MAX LUCADO

Despair is always the gateway of faith.
OSWALD CHAMBERS

If You're Feeling Numb

If you've experienced a recent loss, especially a deep, life-altering loss, you may be surprised not by the intensity of your emotions, but by the lack of them. If so, you should know that emotional numbness is a common response to any significant loss, especially in the early stages of the grieving process. So if you're feeling numb, don't think you're the only person who's ever felt that way. And if you're still in a state of disbelief, don't keep yourself away from your loved ones. Even if you'd rather close the drapes and shut yourself off from the world, you should keep talking to your family, to your friends, and to God. When you do, you'll discover that talking about your grief, while painful at first, can be helpful in the long run.

—⁓—

A Timely Tip

Grief is not meant to be avoided or feared; it is meant to be worked through. Grief hurts, but denying your true feelings can hurt even more. With God's help, you can face your pain and move beyond it.

Notes to Yourself
About Your Grief

Grief is an intensely personal experience. Your grief is shaped by your particular circumstances, your personality, and the nature of the loss you've experienced. In the space below, write down your thoughts about what grief feels like to you.

....

....

....

....

....

....

....

....

2

The Question

It feels like I'm starting over, and I want
to understand God's plan for my life.
What does His Word say about that?

The Answer

The Bible promises that in good times and in hard
times God has a plan for you. Discovering God's
plan begins with prayer, but it doesn't end there.
You've also got to work at it.

*Suffering may be someone's fault or it may not be
anyone's fault. But if given to God, our suffering
becomes an opportunity to experience the power
of God at work in our lives and to give glory to Him.*

ANNE GRAHAM LOTZ

God Still Has a Plan for Your Life

For now we see in a mirror, dimly,
but then face to face. Now I know in part,
but then I shall know just as I also am known.
1 CORINTHIANS 13:12 NKJV

It's an age-old riddle: Why does God allow us to endure suffering? After all, since we trust that God is all-powerful, and since we trust that His hand shapes our lives, why doesn't He simply rescue us—and our loved ones—from all hardship and pain?

Throughout the Bible, God promises that He has a plan for our lives, that He loves us, and that He wants the best for us. So why, we wonder, if God is really so concerned with every detail of our lives, does He permit us to endure emotions like grief, sadness, shame, or fear? And why does He allow tragic circumstances to invade the lives of good people? These questions perplex us, especially when our losses are staggering.

On occasion, all of us must endure life-changing personal losses that leave us reeling. When we pass through the dark valleys of life, we often ask, "Why me?" We wonder, again and again, why God allows us to suffer.

Even when we cannot understand God's plans, we must trust them. And even when we are impatient for our situations to improve, we must trust God's timing. We must continue to study His Word, and we must be watchful for His signs, knowing that in time, He will lead us through the valleys, onward to the mountaintop.

More from God's Word

And yet, O LORD, you are our Father.
We are the clay, and you are the potter.
We all are formed by your hand.
ISAIAH 64:8 NLT

The earth is the LORD's, and everything in it.
The world and all its people belong to him.
PSALM 24:1 NLT

The LORD is good to those who depend on him,
to those who search for him. So it is good to wait
quietly for salvation from the LORD.
LAMENTATIONS 3:25–26 NLT

Should we accept only good
from God and not adversity?
JOB 2:10 HCSB

For whoever does the will of God
is My brother and My sister and mother.
MARK 3:35 NKJV

More Thoughts About God's Plan

*Jesus did not promise to change the circumstances
around us. He promised great peace and pure
joy to those who would learn to believe
that God actually controls all things.*

CORRIE TEN BOOM

*God has a course mapped out for your life, and all
the inadequacies in the world will not change His
mind. He will be with you every step of the way.*

CHARLES STANLEY

*God has no problems, only plans.
There is never panic in heaven.*

CORRIE TEN BOOM

*God's purpose is greater than our problems,
our pain, and even our sin.*

RICK WARREN

*If not a sparrow falls upon the ground without
your Father, you have reason to see the smallest
events of your career are arranged by Him.*

C. H. SPURGEON

He Protects Us

God is our greatest protection. When every earthly support system fails, God remains steadfast, and His love remains unchanged. When we encounter life's inevitable heartbreaks and setbacks, God remains faithful. When we suffer losses that leave us gripped by grief, God is always with us, always ready to respond to our prayers, always working in us and through us to turn tragedy into triumph.

God strengthens those who turn their hearts and prayers to Him. Count yourself among that number. When you do, you can live courageously, knowing that "this too will pass"—but that God's love for you will not.

—⟋⟋⟋—

A Timely Tip

Even when you cannot understand why things happen, you must continue to trust your heavenly Father. Ruth Bell Graham once said, "When I am dealing with an all-powerful, all-knowing God, I, as a mere mortal, must offer my petitions not only with persistence, but also with patience. Someday I'll know why." So even when you can't understand why God allows certain things to happen, you must trust Him and never lose faith.

Notes to Yourself
About Feeling Numb

When a loss comes unexpectedly, the pain may be intense. Or the shock may leave you feeling numb. If you've experienced an unexpected loss, write down how you felt during the first few days and weeks after you learned of your loss.

....

....

....

....

....

....

....

....

3

The Question

It feels like I'll never recover from my loss.
Is healing possible?

The Answer

Nothing is impossible for God. If you ask Him,
and keep asking Him, He will bring peace
to your soul and healing to your heart.

There is no limit to God.
There is no limit to His power.
There is no limit to His love.
There is no limit to His mercy.

Billy Graham

It's Possible to Heal

*But Jesus looked at them and said to them,
"With men this is impossible, but with God
all things are possible."*
Matthew 19:26 NKJV

When you find yourself caught in the emotional quicksand called grief, you may wonder if you'll ever escape the pain. When the feelings of sorrow are intense, you may think—mistakenly— that grief will never end. But the good news is this: while time heals many wounds, God has the power to heal them all.

Ours is a God of infinite power and infinite possibilities. But sometimes, because of limited faith and limited understanding, we wrongly assume that God cannot or will not intervene in the affairs of everyday life. Such assumptions are simply wrong. The Lord is busily at work, constantly reshaping His world and your world. Your job is to ask Him—fervently and often—for the things you need.

Have you sincerely asked God for His help as you begin the healing process? Have you asked Him to lead you on the first step back to recovery? Have you prayed for the peace that passes all understanding? If so, you're on the right track. If not, it's time to abandon your doubts and reclaim your faith in God's promises.

God's Word makes it clear: absolutely nothing is impossible for Him. So the next time you find yourself overwhelmed by feelings of fear or doubt, refocus your thoughts and redouble your prayers. Your challenge, as a believer, is to take God at His word and wait patiently for Him to bless you with the peace that flows from His miraculous healing touch.

More from God's Word

*Jesus said to him, "If you can believe,
all things are possible to him who believes."*
MARK 9:23 NKJV

Is any thing too hard for the LORD?
GENESIS 18:14 KJV

*Therefore we do not lose heart. Even though
our outward man is perishing, yet the inward
man is being renewed day by day.*
2 CORINTHIANS 4:16 NKJV

*I can do all things through Christ
which strengtheneth me.*
PHILIPPIANS 4:13 KJV

*The things which are impossible with men
are possible with God.*
LUKE 18:27 KJV

More Thoughts About
Emotional Healing

*I have found that there are three stages
in every great work of God: first, it is impossible,
then it is difficult, then it is done.*

HUDSON TAYLOR

*We are all faced with a series of great opportunities
brilliantly disguised as impossible situations.*

CHARLES SWINDOLL

*God's specialty is raising dead things to life and
making impossible things possible. You don't have
the need that exceeds His power.*

BETH MOORE

*Alleged "impossibilities" are opportunities
for our capacities to be stretched.*

CHARLES SWINDOLL

A possibility is a hint from God.

SØREN KIERKEGAARD

Refocus Your Thoughts

The next time you find yourself fretting about the future, crying about the past, or worrying about things that may never come to pass, refocus your thoughts on the positive aspects of life-here-on-earth and life eternal in heaven. And while you're at it, remember that with God all things are possible. When you let Him take over, there's simply no limit to the things that the two of you, working together, can accomplish.

—◊—

A Timely Tip

God is in the business of doing miraculous things. You should form the habit of asking God for the things you need. So ask God to begin healing your heart today.

Notes to Yourself
About God's Power

Write down your thoughts about God's miraculous power and His ability to heal your heart.

4

The Question

Sometimes, especially when I'm tired, frustrated, or afraid, my emotions seem to go haywire. Why is this happening to me?

The Answer

When we're grieving, our emotions are fragile, and we should pay particular attention to our thoughts. Our minds are like gardens. If we tend them with good thoughts, we reap a bountiful harvest. But if we allow them to be overgrown with negative thoughts, we reap a bitter harvest instead.

These things I have spoken to you, that in Me you may have peace. In the world you will have tribulation; but be of good cheer, I have overcome the world.

John 16:33 NKJV

Experiencing and Expressing Your Emotions

All bitterness, anger and wrath, shouting
and slander must be removed from you, along
with all malice. And be kind and compassionate
to one another, forgiving one another,
just as God also forgave you in Christ.
EPHESIANS 4:31–32 HCSB

In the Old Testament, we read the story of Job, a man who endured unspeakable suffering. His example teaches us that it's perfectly okay to express grief. Job cried bitter tears; he cursed the day he was born; he expressed questions he could not answer; and he gave voice to his suffering. But he never grieved alone. When everyone else failed him, including friends and family, Job knew that God still ruled over the entire universe and over Job's own small corner of that universe. Job trusted that God was always present, and so should you.

God gave you emotions, and He intends for you to use them. When you express your emotions sincerely, you will begin the process of healing. But if you suppress your emotions or if you ignore your feelings altogether, you may needlessly prolong your pain.

So if you have experienced a significant loss or a profound disappointment, don't keep your feelings bottled up inside. Express your feelings; talk openly to loved ones; allow tears to flow. Even if you'd rather ignore your pain, don't do it. Instead, reach out to the people you love and trust. By honestly expressing your grief, you will take an active role in God's plan for your recovery. And in time, you'll experience the comfort and the joy that can—and should—be yours.

Expect Your Emotions to Be Variable

Human emotions are highly variable, decidedly unpredictable, and often unreliable. Our emotions change like the weather, but they're less predictable and far more fickle. So we must learn to live by faith, not by the ups and downs of our own emotional roller coasters.

~~~

A Timely Tip

Are you feeling anxious or fearful? If so, trust God to handle those problems that are simply too big for you to solve. Entrust the future—your future—to God. The two of you, working together, can accomplish great things for His kingdom.

Notes to Yourself
About Your Emotions

As you consider the way you've been dealing with your loss, write down some of the emotions you've felt.

....

....

....

....

....

....

....

....

....

....

5

The Question

I've experienced a significant loss, and it feels like my grieving will never end. What does the Bible say about that?

The Answer

God promises to heal the brokenhearted. In time, He will dry your tears if you let Him. And if you haven't already allowed Him to begin His healing process, today is the perfect day to start.

There is no timetable on grief work. Your grief time depends on the voltage of the relationship you had with the person you lost or the importance of the dream that was not fulfilled.

BARBARA JOHNSON

It Takes Time to Heal

Therefore humble yourselves under the mighty hand of God, that He may exalt you in due time.

1 PETER 5:6 NKJV

Once grieving begins, almost everyone wonders: "How long will the pain last?" There is no universal answer to this question. Different people grieve in different ways. You, therefore, will grieve at your own pace.

Mourning is a process that cannot be hurried; each significant loss is experienced and processed according to its own timetable. But in the darkness of your own particular sorrow, it is imperative to remember that God stands forever ready, offering His healing hand to you.

The Bible teaches us to trust God's timing in all matters, but we are sorely tempted to do otherwise, especially when our hearts are breaking. We pray (and trust) that we will find peace someday, but we want it right now. God, however, works on His own timetable, and His schedule does not always coincide with ours. God's plans are perfect; ours are not. So we must learn to trust the Father in good times and in hard times.

So today, as you struggle to move through and beyond your pain, turn everything over to God. When you do, you'll discover the strength, the comfort, and the assurance that only He can give.

More from God's Word

Those who trust in the Lord are like Mount Zion.
It cannot be shaken; it remains forever.
PSALM 125:1 HCSB

To every thing there is a season, and a time
to every purpose under the heaven.
ECCLESIASTES 3:1 KJV

Trust in the Lord with all your heart, and lean not
on your own understanding; in all your ways
acknowledge Him, and He shall direct your paths.
PROVERBS 3:5–6 NKJV

He has made everything appropriate in its time.
He has also put eternity in their hearts,
but man cannot discover the work
God has done from beginning to end.
ECCLESIASTES 3:11 HCSB

Yet the Lord longs to be gracious to you; therefore
he will rise up to show you compassion. For the Lord
is a God of justice. Blessed are all who wait for him!
ISAIAH 30:18 NIV

More Thoughts
About God's Timing

*Waiting on God brings us to the journey's end
quicker than our feet.*

LETTIE COWMAN

*We often hear about waiting on God, which
actually means that He is waiting until we are
ready. There is another side, however. When we
wait for God, we are waiting until He is ready.*

LETTIE COWMAN

*We must learn to move according to the timetable
of the Timeless One, and to be at peace.*

ELISABETH ELLIOT

*Teach us, O Lord, the disciplines of patience,
for to wait is often harder than to work.*

PETER MARSHALL

*The Christian's journey through life
isn't a sprint but a marathon.*

BILLY GRAHAM

Remember This

*Those who mourn are those who have allowed
themselves to feel real feelings because
they care about other people.*

BARBARA JOHNSON

*Fold the arms of your faith and wait in quietness
until the light goes up in your darkness.*

GEORGE MACDONALD

*Our valleys may be filled with foes and tears,
but we can lift our eyes to the hills
to see God and the angels.*

BILLY GRAHAM

Notes to Yourself
About Anniversaries

During the first year after your loss, you may find that anniversaries are hard. If you've experienced a significant loss, jot down a few of your most important anniversaries and think of ways you can deal with them.

6

The Question

Sometimes I feel sad and depressed. What's the difference between depression and grief?

The Answer

The grief that accompanies any significant loss is an inescapable fact of life. Grief often begins with shock, then evolves into intense sadness. In time, the feelings of sadness become less intense, and eventually the grieving process runs its course. Depression, on the other hand, is a physical and emotional condition that is, in almost all cases, treatable with medication and counseling. Sometimes intense grief can lead to depression, so if your emotional suffering continues unabated for an extended period of time, consult your doctor or a mental health professional.

I am sure it is never sadness—a proper, straight, natural response to loss—that does people harm, but all the other things, all the resentment, dismay, doubt, and self-pity with which it is usually complicated.

C. S. Lewis

Understanding Depression

My soul is weary of my life.
JOB 10:1 KJV

The sadness that accompanies any significant loss is an inescapable fact of life. Throughout our lives, all of us must endure the kinds of deep personal losses that leave us struggling to find hope. But in time, we move beyond our grief as the sadness runs its course and gradually abates.

Depression, on the other hand, is a physical and emotional condition that is, in almost all cases, treatable with medication and counseling. Depression is not a disease to be taken lightly. Left untreated, it presents real dangers to patients' physical health and their emotional well-being. Thankfully, clinical depression is a highly treatable condition.

If you find yourself feeling "blue," perhaps it's a logical reaction to the ups and downs of daily life. But if your feelings of sadness have lasted longer than you think they should—or if someone close to you fears that your sadness may have evolved into clinical depression—it's time to seek professional help.

If you're gripped by depression, God may seem far away. But He is not. God is always available, always ready to send friends, family members, and healers to help you. Your job, simply put, is to be open to their advice and accept the forms of treatment they recommend.

God's abundance is available to each of us. He offers His blessings, but He doesn't force them upon us. In John 10:10, Jesus promises, "I have come that they may have life, and that they may have it more abundantly" (NKJV). Depression is an illness that robs us of the joy and the peace that might otherwise be ours in Christ. Sufferers who wish to claim God's abundance are wise to seek medical intervention and counseling as soon as symptoms arise. Why? Because healing is available; it's effective; and it's part of God's plan.

More from God's Word

Is anyone among you suffering? He should pray.
JAMES 5:13 HCSB

And the God of all grace, who called you to his eternal glory in Christ, after you have suffered a little while, will himself restore you and make you strong, firm and steadfast.
1 PETER 5:10 NIV

I have told you these things so that in Me you may have peace. You will have suffering in this world. Be courageous! I have conquered the world.
JOHN 16:33 HCSB

In my distress I called upon the LORD, and cried unto my God: he heard my voice....
PSALM 18:6 KJV

A cheerful heart has a continual feast.
PROVERBS 15:15 HCSB

More Thoughts About Negative Emotions

Feelings of uselessness and hopelessness are not from God, but from the evil one, the devil, who wants to discourage you and thwart your effectiveness for the Lord.

BILL BRIGHT

Emotions we have not poured out in the safe hands of God can turn into feelings of hopelessness and depression. God is safe.

BETH MOORE

What the devil loves is that vague cloud of unspecified guilt feeling or unspecified virtue by which he lures us into despair or presumption.

C. S. LEWIS

Perhaps the greatest psychological, spiritual, and medical need that all people have is the need for hope.

BILLY GRAHAM

Never yield to gloomy anticipation. Place your hope and confidence in God. He has no record of failure.

LETTIE COWMAN

7

The Question

Lately, it seems like my thoughts are so negative and sad. What should I do?

The Answer

Negative thoughts are a natural response to any significant loss. But you'll be happier and healthier when you find ways to focus your thoughts on the positive aspects of your life.

Most of the situations that entangle your mind are not today's concerns; you have borrowed them from tomorrow.

SARAH YOUNG

Guarding Your Thoughts

Guard your heart above all else,
for it is the source of life.
PROVERBS 4:23 HCSB

Because we are human, we are always busy with our thoughts. We simply can't help ourselves. Our brains never shut off, and even while we're sleeping, we mull things over in our minds. The question is not *if* we will think; the question is how we will think and what we will think about.

Paul Valéry observed, "We hope vaguely but dread precisely." How true. All too often, we allow the worries of everyday life to overwhelm our thoughts and cloud our vision. What's needed is clearer perspective, renewed faith, and a different focus.

When we focus on the frustrations of today or the uncertainties of tomorrow, we rob ourselves of peace in the present moment. But when we direct our thoughts in more positive directions, we rob our worries of the power to tyrannize us.

The American poet Phoebe Cary observed, "All the great blessings of my life are present in my thoughts today." And her words apply to you. You will make your life better when you focus your thoughts on your blessings, not your misfortunes. So do yourself, your family, your friends, and your coworkers a favor: Learn to think optimistically about the world you live in and the life you lead. Then, prepare yourself for the blessings that good thoughts will bring.

More from God's Word

*The peace of God, which surpasses
all understanding, will guard your hearts
and minds through Christ Jesus.*

PHILIPPIANS 4:7 NKJV

*Set your mind on things above,
not on things on the earth.*

COLOSSIANS 3:2 NKJV

*And do not be conformed to this world, but be
transformed by the renewing of your mind, so that
you may prove what the will of God is, that which is
good and acceptable and perfect.*

ROMANS 12:2 NASB

*Finally, brothers and sisters, whatever is true,
whatever is noble, whatever is right,
whatever is pure, whatever is lovely,
whatever is admirable—if anything is excellent
or praiseworthy—think about such things.*

PHILIPPIANS 4:8 NIV

*For to be carnally minded is death, but to be
spiritually minded is life and peace.*

ROMANS 8:6 NKJV

More About Thoughts

*Change always starts in your mind. The way you
think determines the way you feel, and the way
you feel influences the way you act.*

RICK WARREN

*Your life today is a result of your thinking yesterday.
Your life tomorrow will be determined
by what you think today.*

JOHN MAXWELL

*It is the thoughts and intents of the heart
that shape a person's life.*

JOHN ELDREDGE

*When you think on the powerful truths of scripture,
God uses His Word to change your way of thinking.*

ELIZABETH GEORGE

*The things we think are the things that feed
our souls. If we think on pure and lovely things,
we shall grow pure and lovely like them;
and the converse is equally true.*

HANNAH WHITALL SMITH

Beyond Self-Pity

If you're experiencing the pangs of grief, you may be troubled by feelings of self-pity. But here's a word of warning: self-pity is not only an unproductive way to think, it is also an affront to your Father in heaven.

Self-pity and thanksgiving cannot coexist in the same mind. Bitterness and joy cannot coexist in the same heart. Gratitude and gloom are mutually exclusive.

So even if you've experienced a heartbreaking loss, don't allow pain and regret to dominate your life. As you move through and beyond your grief, you can—and should—train yourself to think less about your pain and more about God's love. Focus your mind on Him, and let your sorrows fend for themselves.

—⁓—

A Timely Tip

Avoid self-pity and renounce regret. Feeling sorry for yourself is a waste of precious time and energy; regretting the mistakes of yesterday won't help you build a better tomorrow.

Notes to Yourself:
Thoughts Are Powerful

Write down your own ideas about the power of positive thoughts and the potential danger of negative thoughts.

....

....

....

....

....

....

....

....

....

....

8

The Question

It's hard for me to talk about the pain I'm feeling.
What should I do?

The Answer

It's better to talk about your feelings than to keep
them bottled up inside. Your friends want to help
you, and you need their encouragement. Don't
hesitate to ask for encouragement, and don't
hesitate to accept it.

*Friendship is one of the sweetest joys of life. Many
might have failed beneath the bitterness of their
trial had they not found a friend.*

C. H. SPURGEON

The Search for Encouragement

*Let us think about each other and help each other
to show love and do good deeds.*
HEBREWS 10:24 ICB

If you're recovering from a significant loss, you need the encouragement of your friends, your family members, your mentors, your pastor, and just about anybody else who's willing to offer an encouraging word or a pat on the back. As a Christian, you have every reason to be optimistic about life. As John Calvin observed, "There is not one blade of grass, there is no color in this world, that is not intended to make us rejoice." But if you're trying to recover from a significant setback, rejoicing may be the last thing on your mind.

If you've recently endured a life-altering loss, you can easily fall prey to worry, frustration, anxiety, or sheer exhaustion. And if you're not careful, you'll fall victim to a sense of hopelessness and dread. But God has other plans.

Today, as you embark upon the next stage of your life's journey, seek out encouraging people and tune in to their positive thoughts. Find friends who lift your spirits and strengthen your faith. Find folks who can help you envision a brighter future for yourself and your loved ones. When you do, your friends will bless you abundantly, and you'll do the same for them.

More from God's Word

*But encourage each other daily, while it is still
called today, so that none of you is hardened
by sin's deception.*
HEBREWS 3:13 HCSB

*So encourage each other and give each other
strength, just as you are doing now.*
1 THESSALONIANS 5:11 NCV

*When you talk, do not say harmful things, but say
what people need—words that will help others
become stronger. Then what you say will
do good to those who listen to you.*
EPHESIANS 4:29 NCV

*Bear one another's burdens,
and so fulfill the law of Christ.*
GALATIANS 6:2 NKJV

*Now we exhort you, brethren, warn those
who are unruly, comfort the fainthearted,
uphold the weak, be patient with all.*
1 THESSALONIANS 5:14 NKJV

More Thoughts About Friends

What is a friend?
A single soul dwelling in two bodies.
ST. AUGUSTINE

I cannot even imagine where I would be today
were it not for that handful of friends who have
given me a heart full of joy. Let's face it: friends
make life a lot more fun.
CHARLES SWINDOLL

In friendship, God opens your eyes
to the glories of Himself.
JONI EARECKSON TADA

They are rich who have true friends.
THOMAS FULLER

Friendship is born at the moment one person
says to another, "What? You too?
I thought I was the only one."
C. S. LEWIS

Don't Suffer in Solitude

If your world has been turned upside down—or shattered—you should reach out to friends and family members who have truly walked in your shoes—men and women who have experienced your particular pain and lived to tell about it. Then, when you've recruited a small team of friends and counselors, it's time for you to talk (about your feelings) and listen (to their advice).

God doesn't intend for you to suffer in solitude, so He inevitably places counselors and comforters along your path. But when you're hurting, it's tempting to pull the drapes, lock the door, take the phone off the hook, and sit, alone, in your self-pity. Tempting, but unwise. A far better way to deal with your feelings is to share them with the folks God sends your way.

So the next time you're tempted to wall yourself off inside an emotional prison of your own making, resist that temptation. Instead, find a compassionate friend you can talk to, or pray with, or even cry with. Consider that friend to be God's gift to you—a precious gift you can use to guide your path and hasten your healing.

A friend loves at all times,
and a brother is born for a difficult time.
PROVERBS 17:17 HCSB

Notes to Yourself: in Search of Encouragement

Make a list of the people who offer you the most encouragement. Then be sure that you stay in close contact with these people.

9

The Question

It's hard for me to forgive the people who have hurt me. What does the Bible say about that?

The Answer

God's Word instructs you to forgive others, no exceptions. Forgiveness is its own reward and bitterness is its own punishment, so guard your words and your thoughts accordingly.

He who cannot forgive others breaks the bridge over which he himself must pass.

CORRIE TEN BOOM

The Power of Forgiveness

Judge not, and you shall not be judged. Condemn not, and you shall not be condemned. Forgive, and you will be forgiven.
LUKE 6:37 NKJV

Do you invest too much time reliving the past? Is your grief complicated by feelings of bitterness, anger, or regret? Do you harbor ill will against someone whom you simply can't seem to forgive? If so, it's time to finally get serious about putting the past in its proper place: behind you.

When someone hurts you, the act of forgiveness is difficult, but necessary. Until you forgive, you are trapped in a prison of your own creation. But what if you have tried to forgive and simply can't seem to do so? The solution to your dilemma is this: you simply must make forgiveness a higher priority in your life.

Forgiveness is an exercise in spiritual growth: the more we forgive, the more we grow. Conversely, bitterness makes spiritual growth impossible: when our hearts are filled with resentment and anger, there is no room left for love.

In those quiet moments when we open our hearts to God, the Creator who made us keeps remaking us. He gives us direction, perspective, and wisdom—and He gives us the courage to forgive other folks sooner rather than later, which, by the way, is exactly what we should do. Most of us don't spend too much time thinking about forgiveness; we worry, instead, about the injustices we have suffered and the people who inflicted them. God has a better plan: He wants us to live in the present, not the past, and He knows that in order to do so, we must forgive those who have harmed us. Now.

More from God's Word

Above all, love each other deeply,
because love cover over a multitude of sins.
1 PETER 4:8 NIV

And be kind to one another,
tenderhearted, forgiving one another,
even as God in Christ forgave you.
EPHESIANS 4:32 NKJV

And whenever you stand praying,
if you have anything against anyone,
forgive him, so that your Father in heaven
will also forgive you your wrongdoing.
MARK 11:25 HCSB

But I say to you, love your enemies
and pray for those who persecute you.
MATTHEW 5:44 NASB

Blessed are the merciful,
for they will be shown mercy.
MATTHEW 5:7 NIV

More Thoughts About Forgiveness

Forgiveness is one of the most beautiful words in the human vocabulary. How much pain could be avoided if we all learned the meaning of this word!

BILLY GRAHAM

Forgiveness is God's command.

MARTIN LUTHER

Forgiveness does not change the past, but it does enlarge the future.

DAVID JEREMIAH

Forgiveness is an act of the will, and the will can function regardless of the temperature of the heart.

CORRIE TEN BOOM

One bold stroke, forgiveness obliterates the past and permits us to enter the land of new beginnings.

BILLY GRAHAM

Make Forgiveness a High Priority

If you're unwilling to forgive other people, you're building a roadblock between yourself and God. That's why you must make the task of forgiving everybody (including yourself) a high priority.

Forgiveness is a choice. We can either choose to forgive those who have injured us, or not. When we follow God's teachings by offering forgiveness to other people, we are blessed. But when we allow bitterness and resentment to poison our hearts, we are tortured by our own shortsightedness.

Do you harbor resentment against anyone? If so, you are faced with an important decision: whether or not to forgive the person who has hurt you. God's instructions are clear: He wants you to forgive. Period.

For if you forgive men their trespasses, your heavenly Father will also forgive you. But if you do not forgive men their trespasses, neither will your Father forgive your trespasses.
MATTHEW 6:14–15 NKJV

Notes to Yourself:
the People You Need to Forgive

Make a list of the people you need to forgive today.
Then pray about your list.

....

....

....

....

....

....

....

....

....

....

10

The Question

When my grief threatens to overwhelm me,
I need courage. Where can I find it?

The Answer

When you're grieving, you should guard your heart
by turning it over to God. He is your Shepherd;
trust Him and follow His lead.

*God is in control. He may not take away trials
or make detours for us, but He strengthens
us through them.*

BILLY GRAHAM

The Pain Is Temporary

In my distress I called upon the LORD,
and cried unto my God: he heard my voice....
PSALM 18:6 KJV

Tough times. Disappointments. Hardship. Pain. These experiences are the inevitable cost that each of us must pay for being human. From time to time we all encounter adversity. Thankfully, we need never encounter it alone. God is always with us.

When we are troubled, God stands ready and willing to protect us. Our responsibility, of course, is to ask Him for protection. When we call upon Him in prayer, He will answer—in His own time and in His own way.

If you find yourself enduring difficult circumstances or emotional pain, remember that God remains in His heaven. If you become discouraged with the direction of your day or your life, turn your thoughts and prayers to Him. He is a God of possibility, not negativity. He will guide you through your difficulties and beyond them. And then, with a renewed spirit of optimism and hope, you can thank the Giver for gifts that are simply too numerous to count.

More from God's Word

I have told you these things so that in Me you may have peace. You will have suffering in this world. Be courageous! I have conquered the world.
JOHN 16:33 HCSB

I have heard your prayer;
I have seen your tears. Look, I will heal you.
2 KINGS 20:5 HCSB

We are hard-pressed on every side, yet not crushed; we are perplexed, but not in despair.
2 CORINTHIANS 4:8 NKJV

I called to the LORD in my distress; I called to my God. From His temple He heard my voice.
2 SAMUEL 22:7 HCSB

God blesses those who patiently endure testing and temptation. Afterward they will receive the crown of life that God has promised to those who love him.
JAMES 1:12 NLT

More Thoughts About Adversity

God alone can give us songs in the night.
C. H. SPURGEON

Life is literally filled with God-appointed storms.
These squalls surge across everyone's horizon.
We all need them.
CHARLES SWINDOLL

Often God has to shut a door in our face
so that he can subsequently open the door
through which He wants us to go.
CATHERINE MARSHALL

Human problems are never greater
than divine solutions.
ERWIN LUTZER

God is in control. He may not take away trials
or make detours for us, but He strengthens us
through them.
BILLY GRAHAM

Ask for Help

Sometimes, when our hearts are heavy and the world seems to be crashing down around us, we neglect to slow down long enough to talk with God. Instead of turning our thoughts and prayers to Him, we rely entirely upon our own resources, with decidedly poor results. Or instead of praying for strength, we seek to manufacture it within ourselves, only to find that lasting strength remains elusive.

Are you in need? Ask God to sustain you. And don't be afraid to ask for the loving support of your loved ones, too. When you ask for help, you'll receive it. So the next time you're in pain, remember that help is on the way. All you must do is ask.

—⁓—

A Timely Tip

If you want God's guidance, ask for it. When you pray for guidance, the Lord will give it. He will guide your steps if you let Him. Let Him.

Notes to Yourself
About Tough Times

In a few sentences, write down your best ideas for dealing with tough times.

....

....

....

....

....

....

....

....

....

....

....

11

The Question

Sometimes I'm overly anxious,
and sometimes I'm more fearful than I should be.
What does the Bible say about fear?

The Answer

If you're feeling fearful or anxious, you must trust
God to handle the problems that are simply too
big for you to solve.

No one ever told me that grief felt so like fear.
C. S. Lewis

Facing Your Fears

Fear not, for I am with you; be not dismayed, for I am your God. I will strengthen you, yes, I will help you, I will uphold you with My righteous right hand.

ISAIAH 41:10 NKJV

From time to time, all of us experience unexpected losses and difficult circumstances that test our mettle. When these situations occur, fear creeps in and threatens to overtake our minds and hearts.

Difficult times call for courageous measures. Running away from problems only perpetuates them. Fear begets more fear, and anxiety is a poor counselor.

Adversity visits everyone—no human being is beyond Old Man Trouble's reach. But Old Man Trouble is not only an unwelcome guest, he is also an invaluable teacher. If we are to become mature human beings, it is our duty to learn from the inevitable hardships and heartbreaks of life.

Today, ask God to help you step beyond the boundaries of your fear. Ask Him to guide you to a place where you can realize your potential—a place where you are freed from the paralysis of anxiety. Ask Him to do His part, and then promise Him that you'll do your part. Don't ask God to lead you to a safe place; ask Him to lead you to the right place. And remember that those two places are seldom the same.

More from God's Word

Be not afraid, only believe.
MARK 5:36 KJV

The LORD is my light and my salvation—
whom should I fear? The LORD is the stronghold
of my life—of whom should I be afraid?
PSALM 27:1 HCSB

Even though I walk through the darkest valley,
I will fear no evil, for you are with me;
your rod and your staff, they comfort me.
PSALM 23:4 NIV

Peace I leave with you; My peace I give to you;
not as the world gives do I give to you. Do not let
your heart be troubled, nor let it be fearful.
JOHN 14:27 NASB

But He said to them, "It is I; do not be afraid."
JOHN 6:20 NKJV

More Thoughts About Fear

It is good to remind ourselves that the will of God
comes from the heart of God
and that we need not be afraid.

WARREN WIERSBE

The Lord Jesus by His Holy Spirit is with me,
and the knowledge of His presence dispels
the darkness and allays any fears.

BILL BRIGHT

A perfect faith would lift us absolutely above fear.

GEORGE MACDONALD

The presence of fear does not mean you have
no faith. Fear visits everyone. But make your fear
a visitor and not a resident.

MAX LUCADO

The presence of hope in the invincible sovereignty
of God drives out fear.

JOHN PIPER

Remember This

If you're feeling fearful or anxious, you must trust God to solve the problems that are simply too big for you to solve on your own.

—⁓—

God Can Handle It

Are you feeling anxious or fearful? If so, trust God to handle those problems that are too big for you to solve. Entrust the future—your future—to God. The two of you, working together, can accomplish great things for His kingdom.

Notes to Yourself
About Fear

Write down your thoughts about the role that fear plays in your life. Are you too fearful? Or not fearful enough?

....

....

....

....

....

....

....

....

....

....

12

The Question

I can't always find time to study my Bible every day. What does the Bible say about my daily devotional?

The Answer

Your Creator wants you to get reacquainted with His Word every day. Would you like a foolproof formula for a better life? Here it is: stay in close contact with God.

Truly my soul silently waits for God; from Him comes my salvation.

PSALM 62:1 NKJV

Your Daily Planning Session

Morning by morning he wakens me and opens my understanding to his will. The Sovereign LORD has spoken to me, and I have listened.

ISAIAH 50:4–5 NLT

If you're grieving, you need a daily appointment with the Giver of all good gifts. Every new day is a gift from the Creator, a gift that allows each of us to say "thank You" by spending time with the Giver. When we begin the day with our Bibles open and our hearts attuned to God, we are inevitably blessed by the promises we find in His Word.

During the quiet moments we spend with the Lord, He guides us; He leads us; and He touches our hearts. These are precious moments that contribute to our spiritual growth. We need our daily devotions.

Each day of your life has 1,440 minutes, and God deserves a few of them. And you deserve the experience of spending a few quiet minutes every morning with your Creator. If you haven't already done so, establish the habit of spending time with God every day of the week. It's a habit that will change your day and revolutionize your life. When you give the Lord your undivided attention, everything changes, including you.

More from God's Word

It is good to give thanks to the LORD,
and to sing praises to Your name, O Most High.
PSALM 92:1 NKJV

Thy word is a lamp unto my feet,
and a light unto my path.
PSALM 119:105 KJV

Early the next morning, while it was still dark,
Jesus woke and left the house. He went
to a lonely place, where he prayed.
MARK 1:35 NCV

Heaven and earth will pass away,
but My words will never pass away.
MATTHEW 24:35 HCSB

But grow in the grace and knowledge of our Lord
and Savior Jesus Christ. To Him be the glory both
now and to the day of eternity.
2 PETER 3:18 HCSB

More Thoughts
About Your Daily Devotional

Whatever is your best time in the day,
give that to communion with God.

HUDSON TAYLOR

Doesn't God deserve the best minutes of your day?

BILLY GRAHAM

Make it the first morning business of your life to
understand some part of the Bible clearly, and
make it your daily business to obey it.

JOHN RUSKIN

Begin each day with God.
It will change your priorities.

ELIZABETH GEORGE

Relying on God has to begin all over again
every day as if nothing had yet been done.

C. S. LEWIS

Keep Praying

Living with intense grief is a marathon, not a sprint. It is a journey that unfolds day by day, and that's exactly how often you should seek direction from your Creator: one day at a time, each day followed by the next, without exception.

Daily prayer and meditation is a matter of will and habit. You must willingly organize your time by carving out quiet moments with God, and you must form the habit of daily worship. When you do, you'll discover that no time is more precious than the silent moments you spend with your heavenly Father.

The quality of your spiritual life will be in direct proportion to the quality of your prayer life. Prayer changes things, and it changes you. So today, instead of turning things over in your mind, turn them over to God in prayer. Instead of worrying about your next decision, ask God to lead the way. Don't limit your prayers to meals or to bedtime; pray constantly. God is listening; He wants to hear from you; and you most certainly need to hear from Him.

Don't worry about anything, but in everything, through prayer and petition with thanksgiving, let your requests be made known to God.

PHILIPPIANS 4:6 HCSB

Notes to Yourself:
Your Daily Devotional

Write down your thoughts about the importance of your daily devotional.

....

....

....

....

....

....

....

....

....

....

....

....

13

The Question

I want to sense God's presence,
but it's not easy for me. What should I do?

The Answer

First, remember that God isn't far away; He's right
here, right now; and He's ready to talk to you
right here, right now. So find a quiet place and
open your heart to Him. When you do, you'll sense
God's presence and His love, which, by the way, is
already surrounding you and your loved ones.

The best of all this: God is with us.

JOHN WESLEY

You're Never Alone

I know the LORD is always with me.
I will not be shaken, for he is right beside me.
PSALM 16:8 NLT

Perhaps you feel alone in your grief. Perhaps you feel like you've been isolated by events and circumstances from which you can never recover. If you have these feelings—and even if these feelings seem very real indeed—you're mistaken. You're never really alone because God is always with you. God is everywhere we have ever been and everywhere we will ever be. He is not absent from our world, nor is He absent from your world. God is not "out there"; He is "right here," continuously reshaping His universe and continuously reshaping the lives of those who dwell in it.

Your Creator is with you always, listening to your thoughts and prayers, watching over your every move. If the demands of everyday life weigh upon you, you may be tempted to ignore God's presence or—worse yet—to lose faith in His promises. But when you quiet yourself and acknowledge His presence, God will touch your heart and renew your strength. So in whatever condition you find yourself—whether you are happy or sad, victorious or vanquished, troubled or triumphant—acknowledge His presence. And be comforted in the knowledge that God is not just near. He is here.

More from God's Word

Be still, and know that I am God.
PSALM 46:10 KJV

*For the eyes of Yahweh roam throughout the earth
to show Himself strong for those whose hearts
are completely His.*
2 CHRONICLES 16:9 HCSB

*Though I walk through the valley of the shadow
of death, I will fear no evil: for thou art with me.*
PSALM 23:4 KJV

Draw near to God, and He will draw near to you.
JAMES 4:8 HCSB

I am not alone, because the Father is with Me.
JOHN 16:32 NKJV

More Thoughts About God's Presence

*It is God to whom and with whom we travel,
and while He is the end of our journey,
He is also at every stopping place.*

ELISABETH ELLIOT

God is an infinite circle whose center is everywhere.

ST. AUGUSTINE

*Do not limit the limitless God! With Him, face the
future unafraid because you are never alone.*

LETTIE COWMAN

*God insists that we ask, not because He needs to
know our situation, but because we need
the spiritual discipline of asking.*

CATHERINE MARSHALL

*The Lord is the one who travels every mile of
the wilderness way as our leader, cheering us,
supporting and supplying and fortifying us.*

ELISABETH ELLIOT

Worship Every Day

While you're working through the grieving process, the way you worship—when, where, and how you worship the Creator—can have a profound impact on your recovery. If you worship God sincerely and often, you'll be blessed by the time you spend with the Lord. But if your pain causes you to withdraw from your church, or from God, you'll be doing yourself a severe disservice.

If you're enduring difficult times (or if you're not), be sure to worship God seven days a week, not just on Sundays. Start each day with a time of prayer and Bible study. Then, throughout the day, talk to God often. When you do, He will strengthen your spirit and guide your steps.

So as you move through and beyond your grief, make worship a cornerstone of your recovery. Let God's transcendent love surround you and transform you, today and every day.

When your grief presses you to the very dust,
worship there.

C. H. SPURGEON

Notes to Yourself:
Where You Sense God's Presence

Write down the times and places where you sense God's presence.

14

The Question

Lately, it seems like I'm always focused
on the past. What should I do?

The Answer

When you've experienced a significant loss, it's
natural to spend time reliving the past. But you
shouldn't allow yourself to become stuck there.

*Don't waste energy regretting the way things are
or thinking about what might have been.
Start at the present moment—accepting things
exactly as they are—and search for My way
in the midst of those circumstances.*

SARAH YOUNG

Making Peace with the Past

Do not remember the former things, nor consider the things of old. Behold, I will do a new thing.
ISAIAH 43:18–19 NKJV

Since we can't change the pains and disappointments of the past, why do so many of us insist upon replaying them over and over again in our minds? Perhaps it's because we can't find it in our hearts to forgive the people who have harmed us or to move beyond the losses that we've suffered.

Reinhold Niebuhr composed a simple verse that came to be known as the Serenity Prayer: "God, grant me the serenity to accept the things I cannot change, the courage to change the things I can, and the wisdom to know the difference." Obviously, we cannot change the past. It is what it was and forever will be. The present, of course, is a different matter.

Can you summon both the courage and the wisdom to accept your past and move on with your life? Can you accept the reality that yesterday—and all the yesterdays before it—are gone? And can you entrust all those yesterdays to God? Hopefully you can.

Today is filled with opportunities to live, to love, to work, to play, and to celebrate life. If you sincerely wish to build a better tomorrow, you can start building it today, in the present moment. So if you've endured a painful loss or a difficult past, accept it, learn from it, and forgive everybody, including yourself. Once you've made peace with your past, don't spend too much time there. Instead, live in the precious present, where opportunities abound and change is still possible.

More from God's Word

One thing I do, forgetting those things which are behind and reaching forward to those things which are ahead, I press toward the goal for the prize of the upward call of God in Christ Jesus.

PHILIPPIANS 3:13–14 NKJV

*Your old sinful self has died,
and your new life is kept with Christ in God.*

COLOSSIANS 3:3 NCV

He restoreth my soul: he leadeth me in the paths of righteousness for his name's sake.

PSALM 23:3 KJV

Have mercy on me, O God, according to your unfailing love; according to your great compassion blot out my transgressions. Wash away all my iniquity and cleanse me from my sin.

PSALM 51:1–2 NIV

*And He who sits on the throne said,
"Behold, I am making all things new."*

REVELATION 21:5 NASB

More Thoughts
About Dealing with the Past

*Who you are in Christ is far more important
and meaningful than whatever has taken place
in your past.*

ELIZABETH GEORGE

*Don't be bound by the past and its failures.
But don't forget its lessons either.*

BILLY GRAHAM

*Acrid bitterness inevitably seeps into the lives
of people who harbor grudges and suppress anger,
and bitterness is always a poison. It keeps
your pain alive instead of letting you
deal with it and get beyond it.*

LEE STROBEL

*Trust the past to God's mercy, the present to God's
love, and the future to God's providence.*

ST. AUGUSTINE

*One bold stroke, forgiveness obliterates the past
and permits us to enter the land of new beginnings.*

BILLY GRAHAM

Focus on the Future, Not the Past

Some of life's greatest roadblocks are not the ones we see through the windshield; they are, instead, the roadblocks that seem to fill the rearview mirror. Because we are imperfect human beings who lack perfect control over our thoughts, we may allow ourselves to become "stuck" in the past—even though we know better. Instead of focusing our thoughts and energies on the opportunities of today, we may allow painful memories to fill our minds and sap our strength. We simply can't seem to let go of our pain, so we relive it again and again...with predictably unfortunate consequences. Thankfully, God has other plans.

We set our eyes on the finish line, forgetting the past and straining toward the mark of spiritual maturity and fruitfulness.

VONETTE BRIGHT

Notes to Yourself:
Making Peace with Your Past

Write down some of the most important benefits you receive when you make peace with your past.

....

....

....

....

....

....

....

....

....

....

15

The Question

It seems like all my strength and joy have been taken away. What should I do?

The Answer

Above all, you should rely on God. He can restore your strength and renew your life. You should also reach out to family, to friends, to mentors, and to your pastor.

The truth is, God's strength is fully revealed when our strength is depleted.

LIZ CURTIS HIGGS

He Restores Your Joy and Renews Your Strength

Therefore, if anyone is in Christ, he is a new creation; old things have passed away; behold, all things have become new.

2 Corinthians 5:17 NKJV

When you're weary or worried, where do you turn for strength? The medicine cabinet? The gym? The health food store? The spa? These places may offer a temporary energy boost, but the best place to turn for strength and solace isn't down the hall or at the mall; it's as near as your next breath. The best source of strength is God.

God's love for you never changes, and neither does His support. From the cradle to the grave, He has promised to give you the strength to meet the challenges of life. He has promised to guide you and protect you if you let Him. But He also expects you to do your part.

Today provides yet another opportunity to partake in the strength that only God can provide. You do so by attuning your heart to Him through prayer, obedience, and trust. Life can be challenging, but fear not. Whatever your challenge, God can give you the strength to face it and overcome it. Let Him.

More from God's Word

You are being renewed in the spirit of your minds; you put on the new self, the one created according to God's likeness in righteousness and purity of the truth.

EPHESIANS 4:23–24 HCSB

Remember ye not the former things, neither consider the things of old. Behold, I will do a new thing.

ISAIAH 43:18–19 KJV

Finally, brothers, rejoice. Become mature, be encouraged, be of the same mind, be at peace, and the God of love and peace will be with you.

2 CORINTHIANS 13:11 HCSB

Those who hope in the LORD will renew their strength. They will soar on wings like eagles; they will run and not grow weary, they will walk and not be faint.

ISAIAH 40:31 NIV

Now the God of all grace, who called you to His eternal glory in Christ Jesus, will personally restore, establish, strengthen, and support you.

1 PETER 5:10 HCSB

More Thoughts about Renewal

God is not running an antique shop!
He is making all things new!
VANCE HAVNER

Our Lord never drew power from Himself;
He drew it always from His Father.
OSWALD CHAMBERS

God specializes in giving people a fresh start.
RICK WARREN

Are you weak? Weary? Confused? Troubled?
Pressured? How is your relationship with God?
Is it held in its place of priority? I believe
the greater the pressure, the greater
your need for time alone with Him.
KAY ARTHUR

The creation of a new heart, the renewing
of a right spirit is an omnipotent work of God.
Leave it to the Creator.
HENRY DRUMMOND

Bitterness Is Poison

Bitterness is a spiritual sickness. It will consume your soul. It is dangerous to your emotional health. It can destroy you if you let it.

If you are caught up in intense feelings of anger or resentment, you know all too well the destructive power of these emotions. How can you rid yourself of these feelings? First, you must prayerfully ask God to cleanse your heart. Then, you must learn to catch yourself whenever thoughts of bitterness or hatred begin to attack you. Your challenge is this: learn to resist negative thoughts *before* they hijack your emotions, not after.

When you learn to direct your thoughts toward more positive—and rational—topics, you'll be protected from the spiritual and emotional consequences of bitterness...and you'll be wiser, healthier, and happier, too. So why wait? Defeat destructive bitterness today.

Always be full of joy in the Lord.
I say it again—rejoice!
PHILIPPIANS 4:4 NLT

Notes to Yourself
About Blessings

Write down a few of God's blessings that give you great joy.

....

....

....

....

....

....

....

....

....

....

....

....

16

The Question

The pain I'm feeling seems like it will never end.
Where can I find hope?

The Answer

God can heal your pain. Until He does,
be patient, be prayerful, and be faithful.

—⟋⟋⟋—

*Heartache forces us to embrace God out
of desperate, urgent need. God is never closer
than when your heart is aching.*

JONI EARECKSON TADA

Time for Recovery

I waited patiently for the LORD; and He inclined to me, and heard my cry. He also brought me up out of a horrible pit, out of the miry clay, and set my feet upon a rock, and established my steps. He has put a new song in my mouth—praise to our God; many will see it and fear, and will trust in the LORD.

PSALM 40:1–3 NKJV

In the fortieth psalm, David rejoiced because God had delivered him from sorrow. Perhaps you, like David, are enduring the inevitable dark days of life. If so, you must remember that the Lord can renew your spirit, just as He renewed David's.

Even if you're an inspired believer, even if you're normally upbeat about your future and your life, you may, on occasion, find yourself running on empty. Sorrow can drain you of your strength and rob you of the joy that is rightfully yours in Christ. When you are tired, discouraged, or despondent, there is a source from which you can draw the power needed to recharge your spiritual batteries. That source is God.

Are you tired or troubled? Turn your heart toward God in prayer. Are you weak or worried? Take the time—or, more accurately, make the time—to delve deeply into God's holy Word. Are you spiritually depleted? Call upon fellow believers to support you, and call upon Christ to renew your spirit and your life. When you do, you'll discover that, in time, the Creator of the universe will deliver you from sorrow and place a new song on your lips.

More from God's Word

*And we have known and believed the love
that God has for us. God is love, and he who
abides in love abides in God, and God in him.*
1 John 4:16 NKJV

*For He is gracious and compassionate,
slow to anger, rich in faithful love.*
Joel 2:13 HCSB

*For God so loved the world, that he gave his only
begotten Son, that whosoever believeth in him
should not perish, but have everlasting life.*
John 3:16 KJV

*Give thanks to Him and praise His name.
For Yahweh is good, and His love is eternal;
His faithfulness endures through all generations.*
Psalm 100:4–5 HCSB

*The Lord's lovingkindnesses indeed never cease,
for His compassions never fail. They are new every
morning; great is Your faithfulness.*
Lamentations 3:22–23 NASB

More Thoughts About Recovery

*There is no limit to God. There is no limit
to His power. There is no limit to His love.
There is no limit to His mercy.*

BILLY GRAHAM

*God is the giver,
and we are the receivers.
And His richest gifts are bestowed
not upon those who do
the greatest things,
but upon those who accept
His abundance and His grace.*

HANNAH WHITALL SMITH

*God loves you and wants you
to experience peace and life—
abundant and eternal.*

BILLY GRAHAM

*We do not need to beg Him to bless us;
He simply cannot help it.*

HANNAH WHITALL SMITH

17

The Question

After the losses I've experienced,
how can I rediscover God's purpose for my life?

The Answer

God still has important work for you to do, and His
plans are unfolding day by day. If you keep your
eyes and your heart open, He'll reveal His plans.
The Lord has good things in store for you, but He
may have quite a few lessons to teach you before
you are fully prepared to do His will and fulfill His
purposes.

———⟡———

You will show me the path of life;
in Your presence is fullness of joy;
at Your right hand are pleasures forevermore.

PSALM 16:11 NKJV

A New Sense of Purpose

We have also received an inheritance in Him,
predestined according to the purpose
of the One who works out everything in agreement
with the decision of His will.

Perhaps your loss has turned your world upside down. Perhaps it feels as if everything in your life has changed. Perhaps your relationships and your responsibilities have been permanently altered. Or maybe your finances have been damaged. Perhaps family has been torn apart. If so, you may be faced with the daunting task of finding a new purpose for living.

God still has an important plan for your life, and part of His plan may well be related to your grief. Your suffering carries with it great potential: the potential for intense personal growth and the potential to help others. As you begin to reorganize your life, always be watchful for ways to use your suffering for the betterment of others. Lend your experienced hand to help fellow travelers, knowing with assurance that the course of your healing will depend upon how quickly you discover new people to help and new reasons to live.

As you move through and beyond your grief, be mindful of this fact: As a wounded survivor, you will have countless opportunities to serve others. And by serving others, you will bring glory to God and meaning to the suffering you've endured.

More from God's Word

So whether you eat or drink, or whatever you do,
do it all for the glory of God.
1 Corinthians 10:31 NLT

For we are His creation, created in Christ Jesus for
good works, which God prepared ahead of time
so that we should walk in them.
Ephesians 2:10 HCSB

We must do the works of Him who sent Me while it is
day. Night is coming when no one can work.
John 9:4 HCSB

For we are God's coworkers.
You are God's field, God's building.
1 Corinthians 3:9 HCSB

And whatever you do, do it heartily,
as to the Lord and not to men.
Colossians 3:23 NKJV

More Thoughts
About Discovering Your Purpose

Live out your life in its full meaning; it is God's life.

JOSIAH ROYCE

*All of God's people are ordinary people
who have been made extraordinary
by the purpose He has given them.*

OSWALD CHAMBERS

*The easiest way to discover the purpose of an
invention is to ask the creator of it. The same is true
for discovering your life's purpose: ask God.*

RICK WARREN

*There's some task which the God of all the universe,
the great Creator, has for you to do, and which will
remain undone and incomplete until by faith and
obedience you step into the will of God.*

ALAN REDPATH

*You weren't an accident. You weren't mass-
produced. You aren't an assembly-line product.
You were deliberately planned, specifically gifted,
and lovingly positioned on the Earth
by the Master Craftsman.*

MAX LUCADO

Find Purpose through Service

If you genuinely seek to discover God's unfolding purpose for your life, you must ask yourself this question: "How does God want me to serve?"

Whatever your path, whatever your calling, you may be certain of this: service to others is an integral part of God's plan for you. Christ was the ultimate servant, the Savior who gave His life for mankind. If we are to follow Him, we, too, must become humble servants.

Every single day of your life, including this one, God will give you opportunities to serve Him by serving His children. Welcome those opportunities with open arms. They are God's gift to you, His way of allowing you to achieve greatness in His kingdom.

Our purpose should be to discover the gifts He has given us and to use those gifts faithfully and joyfully in His service, without either envying or disparaging the gifts we do not have.

JOHN MACARTHUR

Notes to Yourself
About God's Direction

Write down your thoughts about the direction God is leading you now.

....

....

....

....

....

....

....

....

....

....

....

18

The Question

Sometimes I know what needs to be done, but taking action is hard. What should I do?

The Answer

The habit of procrastination is often rooted in the fear of failure, the fear of discomfort, or the fear of embarrassment. Your challenge is to confront these fears and defeat them. Now. Whether you feel like it or not.

Set yourself earnestly to see what you are made to do, and then set yourself earnestly to do it.

PHILLIPS BROOKS

Jump-starting Your Life

But prove yourselves doers of the word,
and not merely hearers who delude themselves.
JAMES 1:22 NASB

When something needs to be done, the best time to do it is now, not later. But when you're paralyzed by grief, you may be tempted to shut yourself in a dark room and do nothing, especially if the task at hand is difficult or unpleasant.

God still has important work for you to do, a calling that He has designed especially for you. Will you summon the courage to answer His call and do the tasks He's set before you? Are you willing to serve Him despite your pain, despite your losses?

It is never enough to simply hear the instructions of God; we must also live by them. And it is never enough to wait idly by while others do God's work here on earth; we, too, must act. Doing God's work is a responsibility that each of us must bear, even when our hearts are heavy. This is the day that He has made. Let us find as much joy as we can while serving Him with willing hands and loving hearts.

More from God's Word

*For the kingdom of God is not
a matter of talk but of power.*
1 CORINTHIANS 4:20 HCSB

*Whenever we have the opportunity,
we should do good to everyone—
especially to those in the family of faith.*
GALATIANS 6:10 NLT

*When you make a vow to God, do not delay to
fulfill it. He has no pleasure in fools; fulfill your vow.*
ECCLESIASTES 5:4 NIV

*Therefore, with your minds ready for action,
be serious and set your hope completely
on the grace to be brought to you
at the revelation of Jesus Christ.*
1 PETER 1:13 HCSB

*Well done, good and faithful servant; you were
faithful over a few things, I will make you ruler over
many things. Enter into the joy of your lord.*
MATTHEW 25:21 NKJV

More Thoughts About
Taking Action

Authentic faith cannot help but act.
BETH MOORE

Action springs not from thought,
but from a readiness for responsibility.
DIETRICH BONHOEFFER

Do noble things, not dream them all day long;
and so make life, death, and that vast forever
one grand, sweet song.
CHARLES KINGSLEY

Pray as though everything depended on God.
Work as though everything depended on you.
ST. AUGUSTINE

The one word in the spiritual vocabulary is now.
OSWALD CHAMBERS

Time to Reengage

When the fog of grief begins to lift, it's time to reengage with the world. The willingness to take action—even if the outcome of that action is uncertain—is an effective way to combat hopelessness. When you decide to roll up your sleeves and begin tackling the challenges that confront you, you'll feel empowered.

The advice of American publisher Cyrus Curtis still rings true: "Believe in the Lord and he will do half the work—the last half."

So today and every day, ask God for these things: clear perspective, mountain-moving faith, and the courage to do what needs doing. After all, no problem is too big for God—not even yours.

A glimpse of the next three feet of road is more important and useful than a view of the horizon.

C. S. LEWIS

Notes to Yourself:
Doing It Now

Make a list of important things that you need to do but have been putting off. Then pray about your list.

....

....

....

....

....

....

....

....

....

....

....

19

The Question

In the dark moments of my grief, I know that I need Jesus. What does the Bible say about following Christ?

The Answer

God's Word makes it clear: we are all called to follow in Christ's footsteps. So when it comes to discipleship, you owe it to yourself, to your family, and to your Creator to be a devoted follower of the One from Galilee.

A disciple is a follower of Christ. That means you take on His priorities as your own. His agenda becomes your agenda. His mission becomes your mission.

CHARLES STANLEY

Follow Him

Then He said to them all, "If anyone wants to come with Me, he must deny himself, take up his cross daily, and follow Me."

LUKE 9:23 HCSB

As you move through and beyond your time of grief, you must walk with Jesus every day. Jesus loved you so much that He endured unspeakable humiliation and suffering for you. How will you respond to Christ's sacrifice? Will you take up His cross and follow Him—during good times and hard times—or will you choose another path? When you place your hopes squarely at the foot of the cross, when you place Jesus squarely at the center of your life, you will be transformed.

Elisabeth Elliot had this advice for believers everywhere: "Choose Jesus Christ! Deny yourself, take up the cross, and follow Him, for the world must be shown. The world must see, in us, a discernible, visible, startling difference."

Today, do your part to take up the cross and follow Him, even if your heart is heavy. When you're traveling step-by-step with the Son of God, you're always on the right path.

More from God's Word

*But whoever keeps His word, truly in him the love
of God is perfected. This is how we know we
are in Him: the one who says he remains in Him
should walk just as He walked.*

1 JOHN 2:5–6 HCSB

For we walk by faith, not by sight.

2 CORINTHIANS 5:7 HCSB

*Take my yoke upon you, and learn of me;
for I am meek and lowly in heart:
and ye shall find rest unto your souls.
For my yoke is easy, and my burden is light.*

MATTHEW 11:29–30 KJV

*Walk in a manner worthy of the God
who calls you into His own kingdom and glory.*

1 THESSALONIANS 2:12 NASB

*Whoever is not willing to carry the cross and follow
me is not worthy of me. Those who try to hold on to
their lives will give up true life. Those who give up
their lives for me will hold on to true life.*

MATTHEW 10:38–39 NCV

More Thoughts
About Following Christ

*Christ is not valued at all
unless He is valued above all.*
St. Augustine

*Choose Jesus Christ! Deny yourself, take up the
cross, and follow Him, for the world must be shown.
The world must see, in us, a discernible, visible,
startling difference.*
Elisabeth Elliot

*Christ lives with every person
who puts his trust in Him.*
Billy Graham

*The crucial question for each of us is this:
what do you think of Jesus, and do you yet
have a personal acquaintance with Him?*
Hannah Whitall Smith

*Be assured, if you walk with Him and look to Him
and expect help from Him, He will never fail you.*
George Mueller

Accepting the Things
You Cannot Change

All of us encounter situations and circumstances that we wish we could change. But we can't. Sometimes the things we regret happened long ago, and no matter how many times we replay the events in our minds, the past remains unchanged. And sometimes we're swept up by life-altering events that we simply cannot control.

If you've encountered unfortunate circumstances that are beyond your power to control, accept those circumstances. And trust God. When you do, you can be comforted in the knowledge that your Creator is good, that His love endures forever, and that He understands His plans perfectly, even when you do not.

Accept each day as it comes to you.
Do not waste your time and energy wishing
for a different set of circumstances.

SARAH YOUNG

Notes to Yourself
About Jesus

Write down thoughts about your relationship with Jesus.

....

....

....

....

....

....

....

....

....

....

....

20

The Question

I'm tired of feeling sorry for myself. What can I do?

The Answer

Look for people you can help. When you're helping others, you think less about your own pain.

Don't waste your pain; use it to help others.
RICK WARREN

Use Your Pain
to Help Others

But encourage each other daily,
while it is still called today,
so that none of you is hardened by sin's deception.

If you're a Christian who's endured a life-altering loss, you still have many reasons to be hopeful. As a believer, you can be confident in your future. After all, God has made quite a few promises to you, and He intends to keep every single one of them. So even when you're in pain, you have a positive message to share with others. When you share that message, you'll discover that optimism, like other human emotions, is contagious.

Everywhere we look, the needs are great. So many people are enduring difficult circumstances. They need help and encouragement; as Christians, we are instructed to provide both.

Jesus came to this world not to conquer, but to serve. You can do likewise by finding ways to use your pain in the service of people who are suffering. As a wounded survivor, you have much to share and much to give. The Savior of all humanity made Himself a servant. Now it's your turn.

More from God's Word

The greatest among you will be your servant.
Whoever exalts himself will be humbled,
and whoever humbles himself will be exalted.
MATTHEW 23:11–12 HCSB

Shepherd God's flock, for whom you are
responsible. Watch over them because you want
to, not because you are forced. That is how God
wants it. Do it because you are happy to serve.
1 PETER 5:2 NCV

Blessed are those servants, whom the lord
when he cometh shall find watching.
LUKE 12:37 KJV

Assuredly, I say to you, inasmuch as you did it to one
of the least of these My brethren, you did it to Me.
MATTHEW 25:40 NKJV

Let us think about each other and help each other
to show love and do good deeds.
HEBREWS 10:24 ICB

More Thoughts About
Using Your Pain

*In the very place where God has put us, whatever
its limitations, whatever kind of work it may be, we
may indeed serve the Lord Christ.*

ELISABETH ELLIOT

Have thy tools ready; God will find thee work.

CHARLES KINGSLEY

*Our voices, our service, and our abilities are to be
employed, primarily, for the glory of God.*

BILLY GRAHAM

*All around you are people whose lives are
filled with trouble and sorrow. They need your
compassion and encouragement.*

BILLY GRAHAM

*When we are the comfort and encouragement
to others, we are sometimes surprised at how
it comes back to us many times over.*

BILLY GRAHAM

Your Eternal Journey

Eternal life is not an event that begins when you die. Eternal life begins when you invite Jesus into your heart right here on earth. So it's important to remember that God's plans for you are not limited to the ups and downs of everyday life. If you've allowed Jesus to reign over your heart, you've already begun your eternal journey.

Today, give praise to the Creator for His priceless gift, the gift of eternal life. And then, when you've offered Him your thanks and your praise, share His Good News with all who cross your path.

When you live in the light of eternity,
your values change.

RICK WARREN

No reunion in history can even foreshadow what
joy we will experience as we see loved ones and
friends who went on before us. We are known.
We are recognized.

BILL BRIGHT

Notes to Yourself:
Encouraging Other People

Write down the names of several people who need your encouragement or help today.

21

The Question

I'm looking for a new beginning.
Where should I start?

The Answer

Start in the very place where God has put
you, and start today. Study His Word, seek His
guidance, follow His Son, and trust Him to lead you
on a path of His choosing.

*Relying on God has to begin all over again every
day as if nothing had yet been done.*
C. S. LEWIS

Start Where You Are: Home, Work, Church, Community

Do not remember the former things, nor consider the things of old. Behold, I will do a new thing.

Isaiah 43:18–19 NKJV

Our heavenly Father has the power to make all things new. When we go to Him with sincere hearts and willing hands, He renews our spirits and redirects our steps.

Are you recovering from a significant loss? If so, the Lord is waiting patiently to give you a fresh start. He's prepared to help you change your thoughts, rearrange your priorities, and transform your life. But it doesn't stop there. He's also made a standing offer to forgive your sins, to forget your failings, and to protect you throughout all eternity. All you have to do is ask.

Are you ready for a new beginning? If so, today is the perfect day to claim it by making God your partner in every endeavor. He can make all things new, including you.

More from God's Word

Then the One seated on the throne said,
"Look! I am making everything new."
REVELATION 21:5 HCSB

"For I know the plans I have for you"—this is the
LORD's declaration—"plans for your welfare,
not for disaster, to give you a future and a hope."
JEREMIAH 29:11 HCSB

There is one thing I always do. Forgetting the past
and straining toward what is ahead,
I keep trying to reach the goal
and get the prize for which God called me.
PHILIPPIANS 3:13–14 NCV

You are being renewed in the spirit of your
minds; you put on the new self, the one created
according to God's likeness in righteousness and
purity of the truth.
EPHESIANS 4:23–24 HCSB

Your old sinful self has died,
and your new life is kept with Christ in God.
COLOSSIANS 3:3 NCV

More Thoughts About Beginning Again

*The best preparation for the future is the present
well seen to and the last duty done.*

GEORGE MACDONALD

*Each day you must say to yourself,
"Today I am going to begin."*

JEAN PIERRE DE CAUSSADE

*What saves a man is to take a step.
Then another step.*

C. S. LEWIS

*Are you in earnest? Seize this very minute.
What you can do, or dream you can, begin it.
Boldness has genius, power, and magic in it.*

GOETHE

God specializes in giving people a fresh start.

RICK WARREN

Look to the Future

Because we are saved by a risen Christ, we can have hope for the future, no matter how troublesome our present circumstances may seem. After all, God has promised that we are His throughout eternity. And He has told us that we must place our hopes in Him.

Of course, we will face disappointments and heartbreaks while we are here on earth, but these are only temporary defeats. This world can be a place of trials and tribulations, but when we place our trust in the Giver of all things good, we are secure. God has promised us peace, joy, and eternal life. And God keeps His promises today, tomorrow, and forever.

Are you willing to place your future in the hands of a loving and all-knowing God? Do you trust in the ultimate goodness of His plan for your life? Will you face today's challenges with optimism and hope? You should. After all, God created you for a very important purpose: His purpose. And you still have important work to do: His work.

Today, as you live in the present and look to the future, remember that God has a plan for you. Act—and believe—accordingly.

Sing a new song to him; play well and joyfully.
PSALM 33:3 NCV

Notes to Yourself:
Beginning Again

Write down a few thoughts about new endeavors that you'd like to start.